THE FRENCH MOSQUITOES' WOMAN

Books by Maurice Lindsay

POETRY

The Enemies of Love
Hurlygush
At the Wood's Edge
Ode for St Andrew's Night and Other Poems
The Exiled Heart
Snow Warning
One Later Day
This Business of Living
Comings and Goings
Selected Poems 1942-72
The Run From Life: More Poems 1942-72
Walking Without An Overcoat: Poems 1972-76
Collected Poems (edited by Alexander Scott)
A Net to Catch the Winds

PROSE

The Lowlands of Scotland: Glasgow and the North
The Lowlands of Scotland: Edinburgh and the South
The Scottish Renaissance
Robert Burns: the Man; his Work; the Legend
The Burns Encyclopedia
Clyde Waters
By Yon Bonnie Banks
The Discovery of Scotland
Environment: a Basic Human Right
The Eye is Delighted
Portrait of Glasgow
Robin Philipson
History of Scottish Literature
Scottish Lowland Villages
Francis George Scott and the Scottish Renaissance
The Buildings of Edinburgh (with Anthony F. Kersting)
Thank You for Having Me: A Personal Memoir
Unknown Scotland (with Dennis Hardley)

ANTHOLOGIES

Poetry Scotland 1-4 (4 with Hugh MacDiarmid)
No Scottish Twilight (with Fred Urquhart)
Modern Scottish Poetry: an Anthology of the Scottish Renaissance
John Davidson: Selected Poems, with a preface by T. S. Eliot and an
    introduction by Hugh MacDiarmid
A Book of Scottish Verse (with R. L. Mackie)
Scottish Poetry 1-6 (with George Bruce and Edwin Morgan)
Scottish Poetry 7-9 (with Alexander Scott and Roderick Watson)
Scotland: An Anthology
As I Remember: Ten Scottish Writers Recall How for Them Writing Began
Scottish Comic Verse

The French Mosquitoes' Woman

And other diversions and poems

by
MAURICE LINDSAY

ROBERT HALE · LONDON

© Maurice Lindsay 1985

First published in Great Britain 1985

ISBN 0 7090 2354 5

Robert Hale Limited
Clerkenwell House
Clerkenwell Green
London EC1R 0HT

Photoset and printed in Great Britain by
Photobooks (Bristol) Ltd.
Bound by Hunter & Foulis Ltd.

CONTENTS

Introductory Note

This collection of work, written since *A Net To Catch The Winds* appeared, is sufficiently unusual in its form as to justify a word of explanation. After the poems which constitute the main section of the book, I have included two diversions in light verse, a level of Parnassus where in old age I have enjoyed sporting myself from time to time. A note about how these diversions came into being might also not be out of place.

Arriving one summer afternoon for a London meeting of the National Heritage Memorial Fund, of which I was then a Trustee, I found two of my fellow Trustees, both distinguished academics, deeply engrossed in serious discussion. The subject that engaged them was the control of mosquitoes. Several methods and contraptions were considered. One academic had heard of a device for reducing the mosquito population—a device the other thought not without dangers—by simulating a noise that would attract males to females.

"There's a comic poem in that", said I, by way of intimating my arrival. There was. 'The French Mosquitoes' Woman' got itself written during a holiday by Lake Garda.

Subsequently, reading John Julius Norwich's admirable anthology *Christmas Crackers*, I was intrigued to find a Colorado, U.S.A., Professor confirming that the female mosquito "attracts the male by the hum of her wings, a fact quickly apparent to singers who hit a G in the vicinity of a swarm and end up with a mouthful of male mosquitoes".

I am indebted to Mr Norman St John Stevas for the invention of the word "leaderene", the general utility of which I have extended by turning it into a verb. For the benefit of those unfamiliar with the full range of breakfast-table comestibles, I should perhaps explain that Ricicles are sugar coated Rice Crispies much favoured by children and adults with a sweet tooth. Were Mrs Cherry Whitemouse a real person, I should claim 18th-century mock-elegaic precedence for prematurely lamenting her immurement. She is, of course, a fictional character who is always with us.

The background to "The Baffled Balladier" is equally occasional. Walter Scott's translation of Bürger's wildly romantic ballad of *Lenore* was brought once again to my attention when I read a German gramophone record sleeve-note. But first, Bürger.

Gottfried August Bürger (1747–94), the son of a Lutheran minister, was a minor German Romantic poet who set out to study theology at the University of Halle, but switched courses to pursue law at Göttingen. He married three times and, as related in my verses, all three wives departed from him, two by divorce.

His voluminous collected works were published in 1778. With so many extraneous preoccupations, it is perhaps hardly surprising that he does not seem to have been a very successful lecturer in law. He died of tuberculosis at a comparatively early age.

The great author of *Waverley* made his entrance into literature through his ballad version of *Lenore*. In that version, Scott reproduces the German poet's stanza form. *Lenore* caught the imagination of ballad-hungry Europe, and eventually inspired the Swiss-born composer Joachim Raff (1822–82) to write his programmatic Symphony Number Five around the story of the poem. Raff's symphony once enjoyed great popularity but, though a fine work, is currently as neglected as the rest of his music. It was my enjoyment of this symphony that set my mind in pursuit of the possible poetic logic behind Bürger's extraordinary tale, with its taste for "horrors" of a kind still reflected, in updated form, through the cinema and on late-night weekend television. The naive conventional pre-television era explanation—that God may not be mocked with impunity—hardly seemed adequate, so in my own re-telling, the story is set in the fancied context of Bürger's circumstances.

I drew upon the story-line as narrated in Scott's version, but I also had the benefit of a line-by-line translation of Bürger's original text especially made for me by Mrs Caroline McLuckie, to whom I am much indebted. If my diversion sends a reader or two back either to Bürger's original or to Scott's ballad—to say nothing of Raff's powerful symphony—it will have achieved a useful serious purpose far beyond my original intention merely to amuse.

Being in old age as in youth a self-doubter so far as my own work is concerned, I sought advice from James Aitchieson, my friend and much-valued colleague on the Editorial Board of *The Scottish Review*, as to whether or not I should include "Renfrew: An Anti-Novel", originally also sub-titled "A Diversion". He felt that it should come out, thinking it to be "prompted by irritation, perhaps even by intolerance, whereas the other Diversions are prompted by a superb sense of the absurd and the grotesque, and some of the poems are prompted by profound affection and understanding". Alan Bold, to whom I had sent the typescript in connection with a project of his own, wrote, on the other hand: "I must say I'm surprised that you have decided to omit 'Renfrew: An Anti-Novel' as it's a fine sustained piece of satire; exactly the sort of thing Scotland (and not only Scotland) is short of". When in doubt ask your publisher, especially when he is also a friend of many years' standing. "Put it in", said he; so I took the decision, since the balance was two against two, to restore the piece to the book, although as a kind of pendant, giving, I hope, undue personal offence to nobody, since its purpose is simply to satirize certain recurring forms of rather silly Scottish pretentiousness.

Some of the poems made their debuts in various magazines and anthologies. "The French Mosquitoes' Woman" was first published in *Lines Review*, as were a number of the sonnets. Some of the other sonnets appeared in *New Scottish Writing*, *Akros* and *The Scottish Review*. "The Clown" was written for Alan Bold's *A Second Scottish Poetry Book* (Oxford University Press) an anthology of Scottish verse for children. "Peter Pan" appeared in *A Scottish Childhood* edited by Sheila Maclean and Antony Kamm (Collins), produced on behalf of the Save the Children Fund; "Impromptu 6: Thought for the Day" in *Portraits of Scottish Authors* by Angela Catlin (Paul Harris Publishing).

To my fellow poets and friends of many decades,
George Bruce and Alexander Scott

PETER PAN

Do you believe in fairies?, the eternal boy asks
as a waving spotlight fingers the darkened stage.
If so, applaud. Self-consciously, we applaud.
A joke, of course. Mere children's make-believe;
for who would hold back time to disengage
the failures knowing secretly forbodes?

Good, good! Then Tinkerbell is saved,
a wish that no experience corrodes.
The children laugh as public adult masks
relax for them, and eagerly clutch the sleeve
of one, at least, secure; their household god:
not knowing who he thought it was had waved.

AN INVERNESS HOTEL

Outside the restless window of my sleep
seagulls rip aside the dawn's caul.
I stagger through to life, pull back the curtains
and watch them scissoring the mottled scraps
of yesterday's discarded human refuse
that waits for shuffling binmen to remove.

Snap-hunting amateur photographers
fall for them every time; puffily folded,
winking on rusty bollards; in the wake
of churning ships, quick dips of wing, long glides
that boast them masters of their element;
or dropping streaks, white as themselves, on decks,
abandoned quays or fresh-ploughed coastal fields.

11

It is, perhaps, their dazzling isolation
that fascinates us, smooth in company;
the rocks they breed on inaccessible,
the death they die an unaccountable plunge
seawards; lonely and final as a plane,
into whose jets they sometimes blunder, tumbles,
a vanished blob gone off a radar screen
that signals for a while our brief concern.

Seagulls leave no trace of their own wreckage.

A CHURCH IN FRANCE

A *fine exterior*, the guidebook said;
and so it was, the soft Romanesque curls
still clutching life, though features that once pled
for urgency had whitened into whorls
powdered with time. Small groups of tourists strolled
vaguely in admiration; others, less
concerned than with the noise the traffic hauled
through briefly intermingled purposes.

A thickened peasant woman, widow-laired,
creaked the door open. Sheltered darkness smelt
of mustiness. A gantried corner flared
its guttering candles. There, the woman knelt
with others fixed in ritualistic pose.

But as I watched, their faces seemed to run
to vacant anonymity, as those
on the stone arch long since had done,
past which the squealing drone of traffic rolled
as, fretting from its tower, a lone bell tolled.

VISITING EXMOOR

We stood, the group of us, conservationists
out to preserve unspoiled the little we can
of wilderness places. Above us, Exmoor mists
unspun their thinness. Suddenly, sunlight ran
through the Doone Gate. My cultivated mind
focussed on fictional passions long ago;
a girl who was never one of her family's kind;
a man for whom love would only have her so.
This peat is smooth as butter, the expert said;
taste it. As I spat out the simile, my far
binoculars ranged on an upturned sheep, its head
sightless though moving a little, a red scar
trickling its milky udders beneath the squat
of a raven. Disgust and a strange fear
shuddered me, till the others' friendly looks
returned me the familiar now and here
that reason shapes, and thought defines in books.
The moorland stretched its distance; silent, clear . . .

Three training fighters screamed across a bluff,
trailing their scorch of menace like a scuff.

THE CLOWN
(A Surrealist Fable)

Drifting too near the Roznian coast
a giant egg got spat ashore
like many a ship before it, lost
between the teething breakers' roar.

From out the shattered shell, a clown
cocooned in boots, loose whey-faced clothes
and straggled orange hair, pulled down
his battered hat and bulbous nose,

then scrambled up the Roznian cliffs
and, though he didn't know it, reached
where neither jokes nor *buts* and *ifs*
were tolerated, since they breached

the ways of an omniscient State
whose citizens by law were free,
though individuals didn't rate
in such enforced equality.

A farmer, solemn as his cow,
saw him. They gloomed the time of day
till, round a deferential bow,
he somersaulted through the hay.

A village politician talked
of hardship for the common good.
Up popped a mirrored clown who mocked
his gestures, emptied thought from food.

Next, waggling hips with mimed guitar,
an anguished pop star he became,
the moment's idol; but a star
who sloughed away his instant fame.

A serious short-sighted girl
called him her hero. Jesting, he
slowed down her fancy's amorous whirl
with pity, proffered tenderly.

Though clowns pretend to broken hearts,
marriage becomes a frozen pose
when there are still a thousand parts
to prank, a self to re-compose.

In each community he travelled
he shocked the posters preaching truth
as State-decreed; with doubt unravelled
their numbing hold on age and youth.

Through that unsmiling land he tumbled,
tearing the shadows from its rules
till some folk questioned why they stumbled.
Was laughter only fit for fools?

The havoc that he caused increased.
Goose-stepping soldiers, trained to kill,
felt less inspired to be deceased
defending dogma's mindless will.

He parodied official spies,
reversing secret information;
turned good to bad, put truth for lies,
thus damaging the processed nation.

Its President pronounced him treason:
This dangerous clown must be suppressed,
or subjects might begin to reason,
and wonder why the State knows best.

So Roznian party chiefs declared
humour a capital offence,
since everything that's safely shared
must be obediently dense.

Still fooling when condemned to die,
they dragged him to a secret place
where, though he never asked them why,
they stripped the paint that caked his face,

the garments that his ways had worn,
and threw him back into the sea.
The membrane of his laughter torn,
he sank and drowned, like you or me.

SCOTLAND
(Threnody for a Never-Ever Land)

Why does our blood proclaim so loud a wrong,
defying definition, like a net
knotted with psalms, that we have snared and set
across whatever thought we'd move along,
trapping us under legend sick with song,
wording our country with unborrowed debt,
a guilt it can't suppress and won't forget;
where only ghosts enduringly belong?
We mourn, alas!, the lost ones never born
of freedom's myth, who might, perhaps, have won
those doubts that left our resolution torn,
the pattern of our purposing unspun,
But dour advantage put them to the horn
beyond the pale of history long since run.

THE BEACH AT ARROMANCHES, NORMANDY

Difficult now to imagine the wading men
burdened with fear and weapons as a hail
of gunfire spurted the still-defended span
of the bomb-lit, softened beachhead; shell upon shell
crumping the ruins of this seaside town;
the enemy line stretched to its bursting zenith;
the arrowing invasion thrusting on,
its crumpled corpses left, at one with death.
A fortieth summer shines; the same sea glints
with bathers' shouts and bouncing coloured boats;
the waves the swimmers breast give little dunts
against the crusted pontoons no tide lifts.
But fields of crosses, the crops of liberty,
stand harvestless beneath this rescued sky.

A VAIN THING

Why do the nations furiously rage together?,
some tribal prophet asked, imagining
his ancient testamental rope might tether
a world at peace to one conceptual ring.
Through twice a thousand years the raging's thundered,
this cause or that the centre of all truth.
How could the blood of man so long have blundered,
throwing at swords or guns its flush of youth
defending faith; a dogma blind and hateful
that can't be demonstrated right or wrong;
driven by fear or greed at its most prateful;
the beast within us craving to belong?
What other creature, with itself at odds,
mirrors its image shaping murderous gods?

A CONVERSATION

Tomorrow troubles me. "Because you're old,"
she quipped, beside a well-trimmed English lawn
summered with flowers; the watchful marigold;
roses whose climbing made the evening fawn,
embowering itself; the loosened scent
of honeysuckle clung upon the air;
a moment plucked from time, indifferent
to those on whom the sun shone, false or fair.
But I have watched invasion's countenance;
terrorists scatter fanatic energy;
bland tyrannies manoeuvre circumstance
to batten freedom under forced decree;
starts and alarms so shouting one man's day,
who might the riderless horse of the future obey.

RETIRING

A leathery old poet, sixty-five,
fashions this sonnet out of gratitude
that here, to be demobilised, he should
with mind and muse and body whole arrive;
his shaping words still able to contrive,
and hold secure against vicissitude
of memory or temperature of mood,
the little of what's past that stays alive.
Of life's quick touch and go he's had his share:
youth and the naked compass of its charms;
music that comforts comfortless despair;
ambition, hung with struggles and alarms;
equipment that he hopes is his to wear
till death's commanding nothingness disarms.

AT DELPHI

I quaffed a sook o thon Castallian spring
on Mount Parnassus. It cam gushan oot
freely frae some un-Apollonian thing,
a wabbit-luikan dug-like metal spoot.
For lang eneuch I hesitatit, foot
upon the haly hill sacred tae verse;
But ilka time I stoopt, a bus wuld toot
and gar me strauchtan my poetic erse.
At last I thocht: *I wullna gie a hoot*,
and bendan doun my heid, gulpit a scoosh.
Ae minute later I'd a soakan suit,
shoved intil't by anither bus's whoosh.
It seems in these days aince respecktit Godes
are nae sae weil-regairdit as tuim roads.

Glasgow Sonnets

THE GIRL FROM NEWTON MEARNS

O Lord, since Thou omnipotently knowest
all that occurs within Thy servant's heart;
and since whatever things are there, Thou sowest,
of blame Thou'llt surely take a little part.
Last Wednesday, as down the street I goest,
I saw a woman looking much more smart
yet wearing just the same as me. Ah woest!
Pretending but to stumble, with a smart
kick from my heel, she, falling, overthrowest
a vendor's fruit and vegetable cart.
The man, without Thy sense of quid pro quoest,
then called me, Lord, a careless fuckan tart!
Forgive me, Lord, though he was not the beauest . . .
somehow I had to pay Thy debt I owest.

INT IT?

Jings! The lites are gaun up in George Square;
an weez jist three weeks hame frae the Coasta Brava,
whaur yous that waants the flamean sun can hava
bo-nanza. It wuznae jist sic a rare tare
fur Jimmy an me. Weez waantit a Spanish bint.
Aa richt wigglan their bums an noakin pie-ella,
but try tae git aff wi wan an . . . senyor! . . . they smella
rat if yur no a creeshy dago. Shame, int
it? An Xmas oanly ninety shoapan days . . .
fur them wi the dirt! . . . och, isnae yon fantaastic!
Bulbs oan the blink an fairy-tales in plastic!
Jist think. If they hadnae goat Jesus born, ah sez,
thaed nivveruv goat the hail thing oaperational:
nae crucifixion! Sez Jimmy: *Yur sensational!*

UNEMPLOYED

Ah clipt an dyed ma heid tae luik lik a burd.
Sumkina coakatwo ur mebbe a parrat,
ma faither sez. The auld fule's bluidy absurd!
Whoiver saw thae things in punk an carrat?
Fur the likes of weez yins wi no the smell o a joab—
the effan burroo an the lass's nippy sodderan—
whaurs thur tae turn ti bit yur frienly moab
thae saxty gloryus years till wur duin an dodderan?
Bit jeez, they noatice. They canna forget wur here
whan we hugger the streets ur stoap at the Central Staeshun.
Pretendan no tae geck, yi can feel thur fear
wur sumthun yi catch, lik the cauld ur constipaeshun.
Weel, sniff yur toaffy noses; jist sniff them full;
it's easier faan doun than gaen up a hull!

CHILDHOOD

From my bedroom window, over a riding sea
of slate-gray roofs, I watched the cranes on the Clyde
slowly shaking their doubtful heads. I relied
on them, mist or darkness, simply to be
there, ridgedly guarding what it meant
to belong to Glasgow: a warm feeling inside
when people spoke of craftsmanship; a pride
that generations long since gone had lent.
Then, on a summer paddle-steamer freighted
with happiness, I marvelled from the deck
as, under propped-up hulls where DEAD SLOW
was ordered by the river bank, a bated
wonder seized me. What storms were their's to trek
that we now passed as if on tip-toe?

THE FALL OF THE LEAF

Leaves break loose and scuttle down Great George Street
as frosted Autumn pinches the pallid air,
their pungency of breath the drift to where
some fifty years ago, I'd wait to greet
a girl; talk nothings and arrange to meet
next day, and next; her springing frizzy hair,
half-hinted breasts and gently puzzled stare,
still distanced promise yearning to entreat.
Now, from the far side, stained with time's defeat,
I smell the leaves and watch another pair
press slimnesses together, unaware
how brief the fruited centre, or how sweet:
and cry my ghosts of passion, deaf as hell,
a shabby Faustus with no soul to sell.

HARD OF HEARING

All that he lost at first were bits of chat—
Maisie's daughter five months pregnant; whether
she'd marry him; what Wullie might be at
if he wasnae sae bone idle; how a feather
fashioned new wonders from a faded hat;
the usual disappointment with the weather;
was secret drinking making Minnie fat?—
he'd nod agreement, needing no such blether.
But skies clotted silence; distance lent
further away; he found he strained to hear
soft music; splashy kindly people bent
much useless information to his ear.
Distorted from the inside, looking out,
All right!, he'd bellow. *There's no need to shout!*

GRANDFATHER AT THE CIRCUS

The smell of sawdust; that outrageous band
oompahing the expectant air as clowns
bounce trouser-flopping jokes, before the gowns
of acrobats are sloughed and, foot from hand,
they swing above a sea of gasps and frowns;
then crack, a trotting sheen of dapple-browns;
or elephants, upended on their stands.
Exciting shapes and colours if you're four,
too young to know the glister from the gold;
a vibrancy of images galore;
but, long before you're fifteen times as old,
nostalgic echoes from a tinkling shore
to us who scent the carnage and the cold.

GEORGE SQUARE

Watching the hunger marchers fill George Square,
God! what a cock-up father's generation
has made of things, my callow indignation
would flash and, stiff with idealism, swear
we'd make a better showing; all to share
the goodies; each to fit his occupation;
fulfilment reached, the rounded destination:
somehow, we'd argue peace out of the air.
Fifty year later, hearing shouts and screams
protest their incoherence - cold and gone
my idealism - violence the themes
despair provides to variate upon,
for you, my father's ghost beyond extremes,
and for myself, I murmur: *Pardon, pardon.*

Seven Impromptus

THE POETRY READING

When you write about Glasgow you only seem to see
the bad things razor-slashings prostitution
streets removed where once the flinty boots
of workers sparked raw dawn from well-worn cobbles
football fields where Papes and Prods refurbish
the mindless slights of long-abandoned wars . . .

The man at the back of the hall paused to refill his question.

fine buildings have been saved and old slums cleared
we've a ring road the P.S. "Waverley" the Burrell
the S.N.O. the Citizens Scottish Opera
the countryside around us still unspoiled
most people never see a fight or a drunkard
reeling Fridays off from the calendar
of his memory they're ordinary folk
as decent as they come don't you agree?

Of course, I said: *I agree with every word.*
In fact, I couldn't have put it better myself.

But . . .

THE SONG
(after the Italian of Quasimodo)

I met a bland composer in the street.
Look, he said: *I've set one of your poems:
I'll bring it to your flat and let you hear it.*
I'm three floors up, I said: *I've no piano.*
He said: *Don't worry. I'll bring a piano with me.*
*We'll get it up there somehow. Then you'll listen
detached, at ease, to what I've made your poem.*
I said: *Don't bother. I should lose ten minutes:
and who could ever get them back for me?*

YOUNG HOMO SAPIENS

*Mummy, it says on television that they shoot
animals—sheep and monkeys—through the head
to see what happens when they're not quite dead.
        Please, can you tell me why?*

Darling, that isn't just the way to put
it. These dumb creatures feel no pain,
and show what happens to the human brain
        so that brave men wont die.

*But mummy, teacher says the dumb brute
is part of God's creation, and that we
must never practise on it cruelty.
        Did teacher tell a lie?*

Of course not. Sometimes nations in dispute
can't settle their affairs, so have to kill
each other with the newest guns until
        the bad are made comply.

But mummy . . . That's enough. Go and compute
the problem on your Spectrum, and then tell
me of whatever future it can spell
        that doesn't scarify.

24

UMBRAGE

It sounds like leafy shading, Handel's "Largo"—
ombra mai fu, di vegitabile—
cool glades where'er you walk by murmuring streams.
But, no. It's what the Scots are fond of taking.

An upper-cylinder lubricant for classes;
poor dukes and duchesses no longer use it,
the lower orders now so numerous.

Some politicians gulp as if they need it
to drown the tasteless rhetoric they swallow,
regurgitated sour with indignation.

It still goes down with those whose prejudices
are most extreme; a dash of laced invective
for oiling self-anointed prophecy.

All poets lap it up; ambrosia
that cures such lacerations of the ego
as being scraped against reality
and wounded in the pride, a place that hurts.

If only we devised a shaping surface,
and bottled it, like Irn Bru or whisky,
the third Scots drink, we'd earn a lot of money:
or someone would who didn't think it funny.

THOUGHT FOR THE DAY

Five hundred helpless foetuses a day,
the woman said in her religious talk—
not soul stuff, but "The Value of Human Life"—
sucked out of careless womb to surgeon's tray.

What an absurdity when each same day
in jungles, ruined cities, ambushes,
dressed up to kill, men sally out of thought
to murder from, they hope, protective distance!

The world's too full already. There's no room
for the unwanted. Praying doesn't pay:
and, don't forget, the young must have their fling,
believing that The Bomb's their destiny.

Some foetuses, she said, *are heard to cry*
before the silencing incinerator
puts paid to the mistakes they realised
but couldn't understand . . .

Switch the thing off!
What right have they to air such sloppy rubbish?
Has she forgotten all of us must die?
Abortion's just the basic throw-away
of our disposable society.

LOST CAUSES

Scotland, the speaker roared, *is a lost cause*.
Having allowed my indignation pause
to gather breath, *he's right of course*, I thought.
But so is everything won, sold or bought;
all systems, dogmas, leaky human laws
that can't make music linger past it's close;
protract the flesh's climax; stoke desire
from cooling to affection; hold a pose
that breathes a part of motion; douse the fire
that cringes scent and colour off the rose.

In from the edgeless cold a wind blows.

Why should I worry if the dream I shored—
a free and classless Scotland—has been lowered
like some withdrawing flag, for the last time;
the daily words I anvilled into rhyme
unfashioned as its liberal values bored?
Now, manic myths insinuate the world;
violence their means, each fevered end
no surer than the faith that Christ unfurled,
a promise credibility can't mend.

Who gains if ultimate destruction's hurled?

Earth that has rolled through millioned empty years
won't feel concern if mankind disappears.

CORNER FILLER

Walking, my collar cuffed, down Piccadilly
I look upon a petrified bronze filly,
a naked hairless man astride a horse
gazing at snow, a Force Nine gale, or worse;
and wonder what the other glancers think
of this cold masterpiece by Dame E. Frink.

IN A GLASGOW LOO

Ah hope yuh dinna mind me speaking tae yi,
sur, but ahve seen youse on the telly? Whit dyuh dae
for a livan? Yuv retired? Yuh wrote? A po-it?
Micht ye no jist as weel hae peed inti thuh wund?

Two Diversions

THE FRENCH MOSQUITOES' WOMAN

There comes a moment in the fate of nations
when even politicians can't dissemble,
as history prepares its future stations,
and human kind's great forward leaps assemble.
Scotland the Brave (oh stars and planets, tremble!),
a land that thinks the world's a football pitch
and truth the thing her players most resemble,
was stricken by a dire infectious itch,
attracted, folk said, by 'a stuck-up foreign bitch!'

A wealthy Scot had wedded to his person
a Londoner, patrician by extraction,
making a Cholmondeley into a Macpherson,
a change that might have seemed a poor subtraction
had she not 'leaderened' each local faction
of politics and charity. So queenly
her talent to devise a course of action
all shadowed disagreement melted cleanly
leaving dull shame, which her opponents felt most keenly.

The flesh of healthy Scots is tough and leathery,
just like their wit and thirst. The wise explain
this comes from striding mountains damp and heathery,
the breeding ground of midges, Scotland's bane
that causes foreign tourists clouds of pain
yet leaves the natives more or less unscarted,
with energy to brace against the strain
of make-believing nationhood, great-hearted
with pride for what they've not yet noticed long-departed.

Hortensia Macpherson (née Miss Cholmondeley),
despite the way her jaw pronounced decision,
had soft and tender skin, however rumly
this seemed to those who'd cleft before her vision.
Although her will held midges in derision,
blown from their flight-path by a freakish storm
down on her garden buzzed an armed division
of French mosquitoes fiercer than the norm
intent on finding flesh on which they might perform.

Their poisoned lances in Hortensia's features
caused such indignity of face and mind
she bought a recent treatise on the creatures
and, reading, was delighted there to find
the havoc all the work of just one kind;
female mosquitoes duly impregnated.
While sex was not for English girls designed
(such Continental vice she simply hated!),
what harm in getting female insects satiated?

She wired to Oxford for a man so brainy
nothing existed he could not invent.
As, freshly slept, from the long-distance train, he
alighted, like a pop-star he'd been 'sent'.
Already, squiggled calculations rent
whole reams of paper. There had never been
such learning to a simple problem bent.
Quickly he built what none had ever seen,
an electronic male-attracting noise machine.

The first time this contraption was in motion,
midges and male mosquitoes set upon
their females. Swathed in sun-protecting lotion,
Hortensia found peace upon her lawn.
From sunrise through to dusk, then round to dawn,
ripped female insects fell to earth in pieces.
Lured by the soft machine, fresh males were drawn,
as fathers fought for daughters, uncles nieces;
to countless millions ran a single day's deceases.

One careless hour, when walking forth in Crail,
a geriatric pedalling a tricycle
knocked down the don, in health but spare and frail,
and left him thinned and cooling like an icicle.
Hortensia arrived upon her bicycle—
she'd left her breakfast urgently to find him
before she'd time to savour her first Ricicle—
suddenly anxious, eager to remind him
to sign a maintenance contract that would fully bind him.

Awakening, she'd dreamt the sound had faltered,
her sleeping ear had heard a distant roar.
Once home, she found indeed the pitch had altered;
a hundred lustful dogs besieged her door.
She fought her way inside, and with an oar,
four skis, a shooting stick, and what lay handy
she mustered all the courage that she bore
to build a barricade, then turned to Mandy,
her neutered bitch, and asked: *What makes these brutes so
    randy?*

Before the dog could answer with the *woof*
it used for all such questions, awful shaking
broke out, and rocked the house from floor to roof.
A herd of bulls had set the garden quaking,
while sweating, rampant stallions started raking
up trees and bushes as with cloven hoof.
Hortensia felt new measures needed taking—
the damage done was quite sufficient proof.
She rang the police. The law could not remain aloof.

She'd made the G.P.O. have all lines buried
for conservation reasons. The upholder
of British rule, though rarely to be hurried,
at once picked up his 'phone, and promptly told her
of what he, too, was an amazed beholder.
The zoo was loose, and elephants were trumpeting,
pulling church steeples down. Insanely bolder,
lions were chasing cows, obscenely rumpeting,
while even he might not refuse some tasty crumpeting!

What happened next? I hesitate to tell you;
but news is a self-propagating carrier
the media just package up and sell you.
To predatory man, the world's worst harrier,
skis, shooting-stick and oars proved little barrier.
Hortensia, in bed a chilling shoulder,
at last learned what it meant for man to parry her,
though not Macpherson. Scarce a second older,
and there was not a virgin left for age to moulder.

Like most good Scots, Macpherson, down in London
seeking his fortune, suffered grief and pain
learning from chat-shows how his wife was undone.
Yet, he reflected, loss may turn to gain.
This public madness must be rendered sane
before he could attempt denied felicity.
He hailed a taxi, drove to Pudding Lane
and reached the Central Board of Electricity
who listened to his plans and promised their complicity.

A switch was thrown. Hush fell across the country.
Industry droned to stillness. Darkness spread.
Trade Union leaders shook the hands of gentry,
both humanised through sharing common dread.
Meanwhile, a local handyman called Ned
went crawling to the source of the disaster
(averting passing gaze from madam's bed,
according to instructions from his master)
and smashed the noise machine with blows first quick, then
    faster.

Somewhere in London, Mrs Cherry Whitemouse
claimed licensed television was to blame
for all the trouble. Self-erected lighthouse,
she flashed out moral protest at the shame
this Scots contagion smeared on England's name.
The Attorney General declared the facts seemed
too vague for prosecution all the same.
Snorting of how protective secret pacts beamed,
the puny private Whitemouse prosecution axe gleamed.

There's some might think we now should draw a veil,
though tougher things than veils were rent asumder.
Macpherson, worn with joy, grew thin and pale;
six feet of his own earth he soon lay under.
Hortensia, enraptured by the wonder
of what she'd dubbed 'the Continental vice',
repented of her electronic blunder
tied five times more the matrimonial splice
while Cherry Whitemouse slept, embalmed in sugared ice.

Scots readers always feel a moral ending
essential to a tale like this, uplifting.
So let us try. Say, life's too short for spending
thought's effort on the riskiness of shifting
Nature's accustomed balance. As for rifting
whatever lute strikes chords that sound offences
to narrow ears, then innocence goes drifting
towards chaos and what censorship dispenses.
Say also, laughter harmonises jangled senses.

THE BAFFLED BALLADIER
(Or Why Bürger Wrote the Ballad of *Lenore*)

1

Old age, they tell me, is a crumbling atoll
round which oblivion's rising waters batter.
A poet in retirement who has sat all
through years of argued undecided matter,
and long since sucked his wounds and clearly spat all
the venom fanged by cheap reviewers' chatter,
can't muse all day upon the fate of nations,
drink tea or gin, play symphonies or patience

while waiting for that silent tide to take him
out of himself. At least, not so this poet.
It's true, he's little anger left to shake him—
though even if he had, he wouldn't show it,
since raging at the dark could only make him
seem foolish and, before blown over, know it—
but relished wit survives, perchance to chime
the past and present into fleeting rhyme.

3

In Once-Upon-A-Time, long years ago—
more than two hundred, if you'd be preciser!—
a German poet had a triple go
at matrimony. This persistent splicer
was G.A. Bürger; pastor's son, aglow
with pious fervour; as a youth, none nicer.
He was divorced by numbers one and three,
while Death stooped by to lift the second free.

4

So Bürger had a problem in relating
to women; one that nearly drove him frantic
since, though a lawyer, all the public rating
his verse achieved proclaimed him a Romantic.
Could such a soul have difficulty mating?
Why, no one curled the latest Gothic antic,
religioned sex, or tortured fantasy,
but his imagination quickly ran to see!

5

One night, asleep, he set out to explore a
harsh memory his adolescence left him.
A haughty, shapely lassie called Lenore,
though just sixteen, for weeks had daily cleft him
with flashing scorn. She was the girl next door a
chap couldn't help bump into. She bereft him
of both his fervent faith and budding reason,
proving that worshipped flesh is spirit's treason.

6

She was the only girl he'd really wanted,
but soldier William was her chosen man.
Freud might have said desire for vengeance haunted
poor Bürger, using poetry to plan
a fate that, had they guessed it, might have daunted
what tracing fingers found and over-ran;
her bodice, then his breeches, each unlaced
and quick delight was nakedly embraced.

7

The poets of Romance, like knights-in-armour
(or out of it, more probably) set store on
virginity. However great a charmer
a girl might be, they'd dub the poor thing whore on
the flimsiest grounds if they could not disarm her
where evidently none had been before. On
such double standards women should be chaste
while men claimed freedom underneath the waist.

8

So Bürger packed off William to Silesia,
where Prussians with Austrians were fighting.
You needn't fear you've undergone amnesia
if you can't think what wrong that war was righting,
or shade a meaning delicate as freesia
to recognise the guilty for inditing.
A King and Empress, fooled by quarrelled pride,
threw army onto army. Thousands died.

9

With antiseptic phrase historians clean up
the ripped-out smell of entrails, dying's thresh
and wine-dark bloodstains, underneath a green-up
of seasons, distancing the sear of flesh
to mere statistics, papering a sheen-up
that keeps the leaders' reputations fresh;
turn agonies that total up a battle
to miniature affrays, a toy-town rattle.

10

An inconclusive truce brought war's adjourning.
To anxious, eager Bessies, Prues and Megs
on tunes of glory men began returning,
some stuffed with boasting, others wanting legs.
William was not among them. With what yearning
Lenore searches faces; pleads and begs!
But not a soul had seen the man who'd thrilled her,
though envying his lot in having filled her!

11

Vengeance in verse is easy, yet it harms none,
so Bürger's pride might have been satisfied;
the girl he claimed he'd doted on was undone,
the rival's luck cut off half-gratified.
Why, every day in Paisley, Bonn or London
such military mites get ratified!
Romantic poets grasp at love possessively,
yet love to hate, alas! just as excessively.

12

Lenore's thoughts might soon have turned to nursing
the future babe had Bürger let things lie.
Instead, he shaped her kissing lips to pursing
blind fury aimed at harmless passers by.
Eyes flashed at heaven, the girl next took to cursing:
she swore that only pie was in the sky.
Her prayerful dad and pious, prating mother
thought Hell-on-earth could search them out no further.

13

My William's dead. I curse you, God!, she ranted
a view her fellow Lutherans found shocking.
God, take my life to prove yourself, she taunted,
then waited for a quick celestial socking:
but nothing happened, though she fumed and flaunted,
for silence answers prayer as well as mocking.
God, Allah, Buddha—choose which takes your whim—
stay wrapped in one eternal pseudonym.

14

Her mother did what all good mothers do;
attempted picking up the shattered pieces.
Deluded girl, what's happened isn't new.
No man's unique; they're one deceiving species.
He's found a minx he much prefers to you,
as different as Germany from Greece is.
No man, however close his ardent wooing,
is worth the pain of blasphemy's undoing.

15

Such talk is useless: wheesht, my dearest mother;
the man who took my love received my life!
I'll not survive, nor dote on any other.
In flesh, if not in bond, I'm William's wife.
It's happened many times, put in her brother;
in war, desertions such as yours are rife.
Of more you'd weary, since they turned a bore for her,
and Bürger had another fate in store for her.

16

Outside the window of her closed despair
a horse's *clop clop clop* came rudely clattering.
Snorting and neighing filled the cold night air,
then oaken doors protested under battering.
The girl peered out, went rushing to the stair
with both her heart and feet a-pitter-pattering;
some difficulty with the rusting sneck
before she hung her fears round William's neck.

17

Where have you been, my own true love? she's asking,
as what girl wouldn't in a like position.
Replying was at first a trifle tasking,
since being kissed enforced a mute condition.
Stood back, she didn't see the shadow masking
his features as he told her of his mission.
The story, quite a tall one, left her senses
muddled as, you'll have noticed, are my tenses.

18

We only saddle at the midnight hour:
from far Bohemia I've ridden straight
to take you with me to our bridal bower.
He pulled her towards the horse beside the gate.
The wind blows through the hawthorn, and a shower
gathers, Lenore pleaded. *William, wait!*
Come, lose your longing bosomed in my arms:
I'll soothe away the world's and time's alarms!

19

Let the wind blow the hawthorn as it will!
Before the dawn our flesh, I swear, shall mingle.
Your bedded warmth's no power against the chill
my stallion paws at and my sharp spurs jingle.
Jump up behind. There's distance yet to kill.
Fearing the fate of mothers who stay single,
she grabbed her skirts with unbecoming haste,
and nimbly jumped to clutch her lover's waist.

20

You'd hardly credit such impetuous folly,
though Bürger and Lenore got away with it.
One moment, she complains she lacks a brolly;
the next, a storm has swept her clean astray with it.
An innocent abroad might murmur: *Golly!*
the story's really gripping, so I'll stay with it—
just like a grotty T.V. serial.
Though less predictable, it's more ethereal.

21

Picture the scene. With neither coat nor hat on,
nor family farewells, awkwardly facing
her husband's back, with equipoise she sat on
the haunches strained to speed the creature's pacing—
and being some months pregnant, she'd put fat on!—
from darkness into darkness madly racing,
pursuing marriage to escape from grief!
Fiction, they say, suspends our disbelief.

So does religion, where what stays suspended
is reason by the feet. That holy mention
serves to remind us; William had contended,
while failing to explain his long detention
in foreign parts, his exile had been ended
at midnight; so it passes comprehension
why, as they rode to what she thought was heaven,
Bürger contrived a church to strike eleven.

Assume he meant the next night, and it's later
than anybody thinks; there's more explaining
still to be done, no evidence they ate, or
relieved the needs most travellers find paining.
They rode a touchless line, like the equator,
it seems, the horse's thunder-hooves not deigning
to print an earthly mark on covered miles.
But journeying has many modes and styles.

Thus, you may use a bicycle or plane;
go privately by car, if that's your liking;
cross seas and continents by ship or train,
providing those who run them aren't striking
for shorter hours of work and greater gain;
or, if the fancy takes you, set out hiking,
assuming that your destination's leisure,
the route you choose, not getting there, but pleasure.

But to our tale, as poets said in past times.
The horse that bore the lovers onward flew;
its hooves went *hup hup hup* through cloudy blast grimes
(a thing that only ballad-horses do).
Hills, villages and towns rushed by like fast rhymes.
You're not afraid? leered William, as he slew
his head around against the storm's rough blowing.
No, said well-bred Lenore; *but I'm glowing*.

26

You'll glow with greater heat when we are bedded,
he shouted back. At which a strange procession
came winding by with sounds the living dreaded;
a *Dies Irae*, gabbled like confession;
a bell for muffled death, not those just wedded;
oaths, taunts and jeers the mourners' loud profession.
Throw down the corpse, roared William: *sexton, priest*,
come, bring your blessings to our bridal feast.

27

At entrances and exits, rigmarolling
of priests is something most of us get used to.
Though we reject their myths, immortal souling
in public is a rite we lend our truce to.
However crude the message they're extolling,
most ministers are literate, and spruce too.
But those who followed William croaked and cackled
like skeletons upon the four winds shackled.

28

Lenore, not unnaturally frightened,
asked what their marriage bed was like. *A board*,
her William shrieked, because the storm had heightened,
with room for both of us, the sides well shored,
the sheets so soft all earthly cares are lightened,
the shape, what men and women best afford—
Lenore saw the moon begin to reel—
don't fear: the dead have nothing left to feel.

29

Too late she wished that she had never spurned
her parents' wisdom, feeling panic waft her;
too late experience's lessons learned,
that what's in store is rarely what we're after;
that much of our misfortune's justly earned.
Remembering how gently William chaffed her
before he'd got his way, she begged his pity;
but laughter showed he thought that notion witty.

30

They rode through glaring streets, a bright emporium
of ghosts, for every house seemed quite deserted.
Most villages by night become a snorium,
but struck with saddled noise, are soon alerted.
This village lay as stiff's a moratorium,
as if from human purposes subverted.
Crowning a cobbled hill, two iron gates
opened beneath the motto: HERE, TIME WAITS.

31

My sands are running out, cried William; *here,*
we bed together in one quiet room.
Inside the cemetry she begged him: *Dear,*
have mercy on the child within my womb!
You've brought me to the farthest bounds of fear . . .
The pencilled moon slivered a single tomb
above an open grave, the earth, fresh-heaped,
at which the steaming horse reared up and leaped.

32

The girl in terror clutched at William's jacket,
which tore in pieces as her final clench
grabbed naked flesh around his ribs and back. It
stripped off in handfuls. In a smothered stench
rider and horse dissolved. One thud to crack it
threw dead Lenore's body to the trench.
By morning light, the ancient mound looked green,
with only Bürger's word for what had been.

33

There's few of us in life escape some fighting:
we've relatives with niggling much too handy;
we're shot at over nations disuniting,
or bashed by muggers high on drugs or brandy.
Yet, truth to tell, there's nothing so inciting
as when another steals your houghmagandy.
However much we grieve for broken trust,
the wound runs deep that mortifies our lust.

It's in us all to seek some other's blaming,
though in ourselves the same dark thoughts are lurking.
In days of yore, one certain route to shaming
was coupling in advance of public kirking.
To-day, we're more experienced in maiming,
know sorer spots than sex for subtle dirking.
Who cares what lovely any man is laying,
so long as we don't hold the stakes he's playing?

Lovers, a jealous lot, can sometimes mutter
calumnies on their fellows more successful;
but crying God to stretch you on a shutter
is risky, though your envy may be stressful;
for you might slip upon a pat of butter,
break limbs, or otherwise make living less full.
So pause for thought among the muck you're raking,
and stop well short of Bürger's undertaking.

Stop? *Stop!*, I hear you echo; *we won't stay with you.*
All legend's false. You might as well admit it.
My answer? Well, I've had my little say with you.
If you've the shape of head, some cap will fit it.
Poet and girl can't pass the time of day with you.
The story's finished, therefore I must quit it.
There's just the Devil left to testify—
and wouldn't what *he* told you prove a lie?

Postscripts

BURNS IN ELYSIUM

1

Move over Burns. Your long ordeal is done:
MacDiarmid scholarship has just begun.

2

If Burns *is* in Elysium, and ears
are part of that celestial condition,
MacDiarmid scholars will be what he hears
competing in minutial repetition.

FALKLAND SOVEREIGNTY

How odd of God eight thousand miles away
to drop a piece of what's Forever Britain,
where British rule must hold eternal sway
for British sheep to graze and breed and shit on!

GIFTS
(after the Chinese of Lao Tsu, c. 500 B.C.)

Most parents wish, before their child is born,
A babe with high I.Q., dear Lord, allot me.
I, who possessed it, hold the gift in scorn,
since precious little worldly gear it got me.
The baby, blunt as an unsharpened knife,
will never feel self-doubting's cuts, the sinister
unceasing edge that pares the tranquil life;
so could, in time, become a Cabinet Minister.

DRY BREAD
(from the German of Paul Heyse)

My appetite has gone, I'll eat no more,
for in my foot a painful thorn has stuck.
Though left and right I look, and both implore;
where lovers are concerned, I'm out of luck.
A little man would keep me quite contented
if he respected me, and just consented
to tell me of his love; a neat-made fellow,
a veteran like me, his views as mellow
as mine are. Put quite bluntly, what I mean
is some old chap who's aged about fourteen.

A SORT OF PRAYER, PERHAPS

As time undoes me for the grave,
dear God, from your supposed Hereafter,
an unbelievers's boon I crave—
let what goes last from me be laughter!

Renfrew: An Anti-Novel
(for Alan Bold)

The characters herein are purely fictional,
so if, for some quaint reason, you may feel
a trifle legalistically frictional,
cool it! Only the shells of names are real.

1

Some pubs—quite why I don't know rightly—
in Edinburgh, get the name
of being literary. Nightly
they prop up the Elect of Fame:
writers whom fashion's then extolling,
in whose direction money's rolling;
others much spoken-of with awe,
although they never stir a paw
to pick a pen up, thought worth watching,
and buying drinks for, since they say
The Great Scots Novel's on its way—
a breed that time has trouble Scotching.
Unfashionably, I relate
a punctual tale that isn't great.

2

Poetry's one commodity
the world thinks it can do without,
unless it's by some oddity
who's found a sexy way to pout
at cameras her frenzied nothings
while breasts and hips gyrate like frothings;
or one who bawls in public squares

the rhetoric of Russian wares.
Readers, if such is what you're wanting
the library will put this back
where Ls fill out the rhymers' rack.
Such epic tasks are much too daunting—
I'd rather set the record straight
before we start, than have you wait—

3

to one whose well-used days are slinking
from Autumn's flush to Winter's chills,
and finds much concentrated thinking
hastens both age and fancied ills.
Ted Hughes holds copyright opinion
on reckless Nature's wide dominion,
while Edwin Morgan and Pam Ayres
have Glasgow's and the world's affairs.
Therefore, my Muse, since you'd be busy,
although I'd rather laze or dream,
take up a plain domestic theme—
what happened to the child of Lizzie,
a wife of three months, who produced,
having been carelessly seduced.

4

Glasgow—a place once widely noted
for manufacturing and trade;
the place an Empire had promoted
to Second City; dull and staid
because of Presbyterian notions—
felt politics' uncharted motions
help folk who bought its goods slip free
from beneficial tyranny.
A rising level of depression
flooded this workshop of the world,
and struggling businesses were hurled
into a murky-waved recession
that neither Adam Smith nor Keynes
had answers for, despite their brains.

5

In Glasgow, caught thus in declining,
the hero of our tale was born,
his mother brought to her confining
on July twelfth (that hallowed morn
when Irish Christian teaching fashions
two dogmas whose unyielding passions
make killing seem a God-like end,
enjoyed by each, though both pretend
their struggle has historic blessing,
a thing historians can't define).
But I'm not one to toe the line
of glib sectarian addressing.
Renfrew the new-born babe was called,
agnostic from the first he bawled.

6

Soon, Renfrew was a lad of mettle;
his mother heired a crock of gold;
his father grasped each business nettle
that wouldn't sting when oversold.
Of toys and relatives he'd plenty,
and on whatever prop he leant, he
could count upon support. Thus need
was not a word he'd cause to heed.
But why waste time on such a brattling,
whom riches spoiled and parents used
to make old friendships feel abused
with boring, boastful childish prattling?
Let's jump the years; to public school
as Renfrew bows to teacher's rule!

7

Though you may find it past believing,
in Scotland, schools called public are
private, their fees each year relieving
parents of what a handsome car
might cost a Company Director.
Yet this exclusive paying sector
once filled a never-ceasing need,

producing men equipped to lead.
Now that our thought's egalitarian,
great talent anti-social taint,
the sinner better than the saint,
stupidity humanitarian,
the Gothic pile where Renfrew went
held values that had lost consent.

8

It graced "the Athens of the North",
as Edinburgh once was known
by men of gravitas and worth
who wined amidst cold Georgian stone,
"enlightment" their conversation.
High thinking never saved a nation.
The activists succeeding them
reached for a different anodem;
riches, derived from exploitation
of captured lands where English sway
encouraged blunt-tongued Scots display
a talent for administration,
leaving their distant native place
a grey, contracting carapace

9

where legal men might argue cases,
churchmen adjust the route to Heaven
to take account of holy graces
for wealth thus dubiously riven;
and where pretended devolution
flattered the central constitution
as ever nearer drew the day
of Scottish nationhood's decay.
Enough! It doesn't do to dwell on
past glories round which fancy shines,
fiction with fact so intertwines
that legend's what we proudly swell on.
But changeless is the clinging haar
that kept our hero in catarrh.

10

Neither at Latin nor at Greeking—
how shall we put it?—Renfrew "shone";
his English and his Maths were creaking.
Only when he was loosed upon
the rugger field did he exhibit
a skill that thought could not inhibit;
the whistle rather than the bell
promoted urges to excell,
as animals obey commanding
when trainers whip their rippled flicks,
performing less-than-human tricks
which circus-lovers keep demanding;
so fringing crowds that roared his name
kept Renfrew pressing through the game.

11

Successful effort's reassuring
brings confidence to those with brains
incapable of much maturing.
To study tiddlywinks or thanes,
and find that some respect your knowledge
gives self-respect a little haulage.
To Man's Estate thus Renfrew grew;
yet he had secret hobbies too.
The one (at least to men) seems human,
the other, maybe rather less.
With chemicals he liked to mess
when not engaged pursuing Woman:
no matter what, or how, he mixed,
success was not the end he fixed.

12

Until a certain Mrs. Murphy—
a master's wife one fifth his age—
finding her urges turning surfy,
thought handsome Renfrew might assuage
the roused but rarely-noticed burning
that kept her shapely bosom churning;
a walking torment of desire,

an icy manner caging fire.
Whenever Renfrew passed, each movement
was followed, though with gaze concealed,
since breeding taught her not to yield.
Endurance must produce improvement,
her fighting father proudly claimed
before the fatal sniper aimed.

13

Matches, they say, are made in Heaven,
wherever that is thought to be!
By less exalted motives driven,
appearance was the *cap-a-pie*
this soldier wanted for his daughter
since eager males in dozens sought her
and she seemed well-disposed to yield
before whatever charms they'd wield.
Falsely assuming she was pregnant,
and unaware that Nature feigns,
she learned that money, age and brains
produce good stock. The father, regnant,
found her an old man, past belief;
she planned to make the union brief.

14

Poor Ebeneezer Murphy knew how
to deal with boys, and stocks and shares.
Fixed in his ways, he had to sue now
for peace against errupting flares
of temper that his wife kept brewing,
for which he couldn't see the cueing,
or find a method to contain,
a straw against the hurricane.
There's little that a man as lettered
can't analyse. But how to cope
with what won't fit the microscope?
As therapy, work can't be bettered;
by school activities year-round
Murphy was calendared and bound.

15

In Spring, a *conversazione*—
oh yes, the term is quite correct,
though you may think it spells balony!—
was held for parents to inspect
the nature of their sons' achievement,
or measure up their hope's bereavement.
In clusters, Science boys sat grouped
when, strolling, Mrs. Murphy drooped
her cleavage, an enticing valley,
directly under Renfrew's gaze.
The shadow trapped him in a daze,
unsure if it was chance or sally
that brought about the brief exchange
inviting more than eyes to range.

16

When guests and pupils had departed,
bewildered Renfrew lingered on;
into his heart desire had darted,
for once, not fired by Miss Anon.
The married she who was the cause of it
sneaked back, unmindful of the laws of it.
Careless of reputation's check
she threw herself at Renfrew's neck.
Exploring, soon his hands uncovered
the longing fondled in her breasts;
and, after brief caressing tests,
no longer round her skirt-edge hovered.
Thus, one thing leads up to another:
in just nine months she was a mother.

17

Modest by nature, and retiring,
detail, you'll notice, I've compressed.
Excitement had the pair perspiring
when only partially undressed.
A glue designed to counter sniffing
was knocked by Renfrew's elbow, scliffing
silk stockings of the finest mesh

where they encased still hidden flesh.
There's nothing makes a woman madder,
or switch into a fouler mood,
emitting words no lady should,
than stockings that unfurl a ladder.
He might have got a blackened eye
had not his hand advanced so high.

18

Yet sometimes Providence looks kindly
on those who serve true loving's cause.
Renfrew's invention seeped out blindly
while they embraced fond Nature's laws.
However all-consuming passion,
convention, and its ally, fashion,
decrees that lovers must be clad
when not engaged in being had.
Out from her crumpled scraps of clothing
Renfrew had lately tossed aside—
though drowsy still, and satisfied—
she plucked her stockings, softly oathing,
But lo! the ladder had unrun
beneath the web the glue had spun.

19

Strange as it seems, the word *Eureka*:
was what Pru Murphy first exclaimed.
Renfrew, she urged, *we'll quickly seek a
patent*. The boy, still half-inflamed
with passion, noticing the curtain
had not been drawn, said: *Let's make certain*:
And, laying her upon the floor
from the beginning tried once more.
This time, his ardour's eager ripping
rung ladders down from knee to toe.
Once more this cause of woman's woe
was halted by the beaker dripping.
A future's ours, cried Pru, arising;
a statement Renfrew found surprising.

20

For Murphy, from the open doorway
amazement tempering his wrath,
in what he fancied was a whore way,
like Venus from the sea's cold bath
saw Pru emerge from her employment
flushed pink with love and greed's enjoyment;
so, trained to classical constraint,
he promptly dropped into a faint.
Thus trapped, the happy flagrant couple
stole softly out across the night,
frightened, yet feeling uncontrite,
dressing while running, being supple.
When Murphy woke, Pru's misdemeaning
seemed but a figment of his dreaming.

21

Now Pru had quite a clever head on;
at calculating, more than fair,
though beautiful, and good to bed on,
a clutch of gifts though somewhat rare.
She analysed the glue's prescription
and patented a full description
protected by the name PRUREN
to keep it safe from rival's ken.
With money that her late Dad gave her
when she to Murphy had been joined,
a business partnership she coined,
not thinking Renfrew still might crave her.
They bought a factory. Soon, they found
it prospered, doubling pound for pound.

22

While thus engaged in secret fixing,
strictly she made herself adept
at claiming business not for mixing
with pleasure. Renfrew thus was kept
at arm's-length, though his days of schooling
had finished as their ledger's ruling
saw multiplying profits soar.

While sudden wealth may often pour
on wounded pride some consolation,
for satisfaction when you're young
philosophy's a poor foundation.
Though fate held Pru and Renfrew roped,
he never got for what he hoped.

23

Harsh fate had other things in waiting.
While Murphy, with unfeigned delight
saw shares in PRUREN raise their rating,
a blessing came to him one night
just two months from his fainting stumble.
In bed with Pru he'd sometimes fumble
in brief attempts to gratify.
When softly to herself she'd cry
he'd wish himself five decades younger
to meet the challenge of love's arts;
yet suddenly, his withered parts
seemed to arouse her questing hunger.
But it was Renfrew's classroom deed
that brought about this urgent need.

24

In these days, having an abortion
instead of taking previous care
was thought an evil soul-contortion,
expensive, dangerous and rare.
Of all the common ills that eat us
none's as malignant as the foetus
implanted in a thoughtless womb
not put there by a husband's plume.
Finding her late spontaneous mating
left more than married coupling could,
hopeful, she coaxed and sucked and chewed
to legalise her propagating.
Old fiddles play the sweetest tunes
thought Murphy in his pantaloons.

So sweet that, two months prematurely,
the child he'd not begotten leapt
into the world, and was securely
christened Murphy. Renfrew wept
inside to see what he'd created
to pedantry thus dedicated.
But there was little he could do.
For eighteen months the baby grew,
then Nature introduced fresh trouble.
Upon the beaming toddler's face
one glance, beyond all doubt, could trace
features too clearly Renfrew's double.
Pru's mother noticed, and remarked,
not guessing what a fire she'd sparked.

26

Renfrew undaunted by persuasion,
bided his time till he could seize
upon a suitable occasion
to thaw his passion from the freeze
that well-named Prudence had imposed,
less deeply than she still supposed.
Murphy, though outwardly alive,
was deemed, on reaching eighty-five,
no longer fit to render Latin
intelligibly, week by week,
nor flesh the bones of ancient Greek
in classrooms which they slept, not sat in.
The tardy governors then mentioned,
since Death held back, he might be pensioned.

Determined that his son's upbringing
should know a father's guiding hand,
one morning, when Assembly singing
had ended, and the word *Disband*
been uttered by the stern headmaster,
what not the highest paid forecaster
could ever have foreseen occurred.

A swivelling commotion stirred
as Renfrew, with excited finger
stabbing the air around the dais
ranted at Murphy. *What I say is,
I fathered that man's child!* To linger
he had no chance. With hefty bounce
two rugger masters launched their pounce.

28

There then ensued a schoolboy babel
we'd best forget. A handy glove
would once have slapped a cheek. Unable
to strike revenge, poor Murphy drove
to see his lawyer. Quick divorcing
he asked for, bony fists enforcing
upon the legal man's man's cool say
in urging caution and delay.
Prudence, enraged at this betrayal,
decided she'd defend the case.
Death edged the plaintiff from his place
with scarce a week to the assayal.
The rescued lady promptly turned
on Renfrew. Mocked, reviled and spurned,

29

he reeled in stricken, sad amazement,
that she who once had granted all
should now require complete abasement
as payment for that fruitful fall.
Yet those who reach to passion's limit
find later anger may not dim it;
they've spent a portion of their life
they can't get back. Thus, many a wife
has come to rue the sharp contusion
of words and wills that led to Court;
however strong her new support,
found law can't separate that fusion;
and nothing's left for love but faking
the memory of her first taking.

You're thinking that I've quite forgotten
Murphy, the first of men she knew.
I doubt if I would bet a lot on
whatever Murphy got to do.
The difference between such fumbling
and Renfrew's rapturous, mad tumbling
takes care of that. About this point
I ought to throw things out of joint,
if Cousin Bute or Uncle Cowal
or Brother Lanark set the style,
with autobiographic byle
let out a long anarchic howl,
revealing on self-conscious shoulders
small chips that rub as if they're boulders.

Yes, yes! I know the last two stanzas
have endings weekly feminine.
The story isn't Aunt Lochranza's
and certainly it won't be mine;
(though that may stop it winning prizes—
away! vainglorious surmises).
When Renfrew saw he wouldn't die
of grieving, it was not Versailles,
Vienna or Hong Kong, but London
that welcomed his frustrated frame,
revenge against The Sex his game,
intent on leaving nothing undone.
(Observe that I no longer stray
from rhyming in the proper way.)

Yet, being gallant, kind and gracious,
in both our interests I spare
you details, lest I'm thought salacious.
Suffice to say that I'm aware
both cunnilingus and fellatio
(although I wouldn't know the ratio)
he practised, finding simple sex

almost so boring as to vex
an expert on what's thought perversion
by some; by others, justified—
if antique authors haven't lied:—
since done by Roman, Greek and Persian
for whom these pleasures proved delight
achieved through willingness, not fright.

33

So Renfrew thought, yet soon discovered
that sex cajoled for, hired or bought
turns meaningless; that women lovered
for quick investment yielded nought.
His spirits sank, thus overtaken
by bleak despair. He felt forsaken,
his manhood chilling with the cold
that numbs the blood of those grown old,
although his road to desperation
was mileaged through a single year.
But haughty Prudence claims your ear,
our sub-plot needing some narration,
though we'll not leave the roué long
since right should triumph over wrong.

34

Prudence encountered Arthur Sparwell
who led the Stocking-Makers' Guild;
atomic as the whole of Harwell,
the post less than the man it filled.
With stockings Arthur sought to strangle
the bosses' power from every angle,
distorting words to tie each knot.
All signed agreements seemed a plot
to Arthur's fierce imagination,
collective bargaining on pay
while working through an honest day:
sheer foolishness; downright stagnation;
a threat to just Society:
he claimed without dubiety.

35

One morning, Arthur's little gaggle
of bully-boys breenged through the door.
Prudence with Arthur tried to haggle
as work was halted on the floor
while shop stewards called a hasty meeting,
dubbing the product job-defeating.
It ended with a cheering shout
that shaped to: *Everybody out*.
The principle of obsolescence
must come before that lesser plight
all governments have failed to fight—
the sick economy's tumescence:
or rather, fought, but couldn't cure,
faith, hope and dogma all unsure.

36

Stockings, the stewards declared, must ladder;
employment was their first concern.
Prudence—enraged, enlightened, saddened—
cut short their cackle. Primly, stern,
she hoped they'd find that unemployment
would prove as heady an enjoyment
as sabbotage, then promptly swore
the factory would stock no more.
Arthur exploded screaming headlines—
he'd bargain freely, like for like—
urging the nation go on strike
if Prudence wouldn't meet his deadlines,
conceding all his just demands:
but both rejected these commands.

37

A southward telemessage winging
reached he whom once she'd thought a dunce,
her temper and her ears both ringing:
All is forgiven. Come at once.
Through lengthened hours, while she awaited
reply, at last she contemplated
the price that Renfrew might demand;

at last began to understand
life offers more than women's libbing
when partnership's complete and free;
except through Nature's fealty,
a girl's no longer Adam's ribbing.
As trunk for semmit, foot for shoe,
there's things that only two can do.

38

Dulled by accustomed disillusion,
Renfrew received the summons, sacked
the whore he'd slept with, felt confusion
assail him, though he quickly packed
the things he'd need as a weekender,
his dissipating monthslong bender
so weakening his usual strength
he couldn't visualise the length
of stay that Pru anticipated.
Adversity may clear the mind,
revalue much that's good or kind
though previously underrated.
Of these warm influences, not
the merest inkling Renfrew got.

39

Imagine, therefore, how surprising
he found it when the London plane
disgorged him, still not realising
how pleasure may be born of pain.
Advancing to the final barrier
as fleet of foot as any harrier,
he saw the sexy creature beam
the welcome of a longed-for dream.
A few short steps, and her embracing
was perfumed promise, with a flow
of: *Now I'll never let you go:*
and: *Dearest darling:* quite effacing
the memory of those he'd laid
beneath him, having duly paid.

40

If you expect me to undress them
at this late stage, the answer's *no*.
Oblivion will soon caress them
as into married life they go.
I've spaced the sex throughout these pages
according to best-selling sages;
of money's-worth you've had enough.
The story's done; I'll shed the slough.
Arthur went searching further battles:
the couple turned out plastic toys;
dolls for the girls and guns for boys,
while for the babies, space-age rattles
that shot through Britain's trade eclipse,
outselling whisky, cars and ships.

41

Their union in a listed abbey,
was dubbed the wedding of the year,
Renfrew's hired frock-coat slightly shabby,
Prudence, emblossomed, satined sheer
beneath her virgin lace, beguiling,
yet wreathed in enigmatic smiling
that made some wonder how the pair
in married partnership might fare.
So, were they happy ever after?
Doubtless they shed their share of tears,
knew tiffs and triumphs, hopes and fears.
Yet lasting love needs present laughter.
Were they with that cementing blessed?—
Your answer's just as I'd have guessed!

42

Novels should have a moral ending,
the hero's passion deeply quenched;
or each to separation wending
as readers' handkerchiefs get drenched;
or safely snuggled up together,
emotion-proofed inside their tether;
or, having clutched and clenched and kissed,

fade into film-like choral mist.
But in a place-named anti-novel
such niceties have little part:
the reader knows the author's heart
is disengaged, and so won't grovel
to scoop a brief newsworthy shout
in hopes of shaking lucre out.

43

To blurb-digesting cub reviewers
my story-line may seem absurd;
to avid television viewers,
quite strong compared to what they've heard
in so-called situation drama;
that boring nightly panorama
of coloured continents and seas
where mindless violence seeks to please.
In Scotland, where we seem heroic
whenever thinking of ourselves,
the native books that groan our shelves
must show our cut; severely stoic;
a race of macho-thrusting men
with football, women, prayer and pen.

44

More than my tale is past believing!
A nation perched upon the fence;
its postured toughness, self-deceiving;
its bluff ignored; its claims, pretence;
its heritage, one long sub-edit;
a spent account bereft of credit.
Proppers of pubs, the hour is late;
much has been sunk; wipe clean the slate.
There's nothing great about declension;
our common plight is what abides.
Let's fight what threatens and divides,
produce the goods and chance dimension.
So, clink a double toast with me—
Scotland—with love and irony!

61